The End Of America

Book Three

Acknowledgments

Some of these poems have appeared in *Abraham Lincoln* and *Eleven Eleven*. Thanks to the editors.

The End of America, Book Three

Design by Adam Deutsch

First Edition
ISBN: 978-1-943899-08-1

The End
Of America

Book Three

Mark Wallace

Cut off   going towards what's gone behind
         freeway laboratory debacle   you mean who
                                                     with that?

                         Information "out there"
                         headache "in here"
lollipop over the looseness   stamina removed
         median house $489,000

"Could deal with three, never saw number four"
regional bias of walking down the street
under an assumed name
                         throbbing all over
                         "looking for an edge"

         waving his arms, n'est-ce pas?
                                        I can't not not
do what you're not telling me not to not do

         rising role of paying respect   ah blue flower
                         forensic slapbuck inheritance

         Where the wild things
                         sample goods   otherworldly incident
"this blue piece of charcoal   for which people have murdered"
monthly moment of slander
                         intimate bird poop
         gently stepping up   like, this is like, like

"I could be more thoughtful without the flamethrower"
                 fear of the tiny ornament
we'll have no, none, loving right into the order
                 don't tell me   please

always someone offended before anything happens
         mood of a bayou
                         a beach
                         late night train

to faraway romantic auras
what makes them lovely?
lonely?
and what would it mean to say they are lovely
to whom or think it and not be able not to not to say it

parking lots from hills to the sea   ah available parking
one more distance / distaste

*

Backlash, then backlash   taken downstairs in handcuffs
housing market crash   test venture vulture
a little tic, grabbing the skin on my neck
can I lose in this instant when thinking it
          I think so   pound to euro   dollar to pound
said to be happening   Islamic terrorists head deep
into wild San Diego County
do you only have urges that you approve of?
Feeding habits of moles and Protestants
major advancements in animal programming
never saw the change-up   heuristic voyeur
Price Ioncon and Associates Inc
what do you want I mean   sovereignty of kisses
official forum on restrictions of touch
the rat trap functions how?
Diverse misunderstanding   convenient bins
ah sock ah puppet ah need to cool down
"you can't just renege"   consistently urgent
internet comment phone call chatter   anything anything
why no one has to care
take one more   add hallway gossip
to be baboon or on the run   quality flak
another language I don't speak
mirror of limits   young woman broods by a wall
top-heavy style
retirees, the military, real estate salespeople, cops

extend maximum mortgage returns
no street to walk down anymore
to need help or give it or need it and give it

*

Real stories of real people doing real things
smashed leg diabetes a tendency to shout
make the quick switch in insurance provider
          seeking education   concrete feel of concrete
cost of a little suburban hideaway
or always choosing Turnstile Three
about 500 men directly responsible
star maker   mistake
                                        just a little pander
a bump on the head   "like the whole world"
mucho feedback, bundled ear
          usual sets of clichés about spies
you twist it, it twists back   moratorium
                                        on stashing assets
          "blamed a couple Filipinos"
time to straighten your hero priorities
in the cash box?
                    Primness of mind
all over the matter, time to rock out
when pay day hurts

I know not feeling is where you want me
like you look at some people and say "Who cares?"
all over the banister
"Doesn't mean nothin' to a man in a cubicle"
want a better gateway drug
to get under these layers of dumbfounded sensitive
retrievable units farmed out to industry
to wake up and find you've become the cash cow
of a hardcore trader to determined to milk it
who kneeled down and killed my Forbes 500

among the last bits of undeveloped shoreline
inside the military base

*

Could be counted on to kill
his own interests
committee meetings and the death of the mind
instant feedback computer clicker
office   highway   town   apartment
fried chicken is a burger
stairs lead up to a missing building
not willing to hear that information
bucket, never filled
an instant of art on hallway walls
her eyes squint as she reports
get my cell my
sense of being special
deforestation climate change accelerated species loss
this chance to kiss on the bleachers
vanished into a ravenous
wish not to care   "Minds of the Snipers Revealed"
compact data pack on sale
anything they could find about
the lack of need for hands   all over television
put the goods on the table now what
deed did you have   "in mind"
urgency in quiet
kitchen with gleaming appliances
"a scene, I wanted a scene"
          like dogs
walk down the beach? no negotiation even
so close to draw a profile of
working for weeks on the hospital contract
a bigger world "over there"   "free sandwich, free
the youth thrown away on commercials"
the ultimate penalty the state has to offer

no devices no questions nothing
about what happened   no sheer benevolence
no on camera interview
like if there was a point
to the sensory barrage we go
over it again

can't move to Bolinas can't stay here
first time since the shocking
halt

*

Fires are leaping
through neighborhoods and you
want feelings? Like connection
to dreams of what could happen
reverse call 911 malfunction
in-town hothouse? Hopelessness, cheerful,
feels more hopeful than orchestrated hope
spooked lab rat disrupting condolences
on stage in front of media vans.
Explain yourself and not be
angry anymore

*

This interregnum
can't leave the noise out
maybe I don't want
your cut rate holy relic
in my rain barrel
I'm not that kind
of man forever again

*

Zombie Chipotle   on every corner a profit motive
wanted in the muck?
                         Can't scare no one with
that feedback tale do you
know where to be born to feel
there's no story to hold it
          I live in this house, see   have to learn
the First Alleviation Response Team Codebook
before I hit Atlanta   daily log
of why not to push you away so that
nothing in the world   touches
to produce a random surge
no longer in the casket   what's the meaning of
this housing development intrusion
                         future one world cash bar
wanna go?
                    Another century of self
under smoky skies   bits of ash falling
on car hoods sidewalks balconies
surely we heard from inside the door
"what greater destiny than serving me"
no threat from gas?   no independent brain work?
Could be the way it all moved
or open sea rolling heavy to shore
anything's better than standing around
                              Time
for strangers maybe to wander
          left behind left out left over
all my estate both personal and real
in the bushes
life as a series of discrete
ways not to just see it all over again
or conceal the evidence
of locked up incidents, wanting my government back
and glad to be suspected

                         *

master dinner is served

*

a furious squall comes up
in my chest

*

flecks of wood   clear plastic wrap splinters
fall from the clouds, cover the balcony and car
red skies drop our century on us
what goes up etc.

*

Always rushing the exit   verbal miscue
half-thought canard
blows back your hairy featureless fussbudget
parlor game got the Nyquil
          "one death in life please: medicated"
"aw yeah" from rafters   to not be like any
thing you're part of   defensively
not good   quiet joys of debate
someone might actually think you're a
          why bother to finish that

around the corner it really bears down

another way to mispronounce "home"
can I buy, then combine   o someone's name I'm
not another replaceable disk
                    except alternate Mondays
my hands in the juvenilia
                              Jam that
feedback through the required receptacle

in hilarity's "who got more attention?"
conservation tip-off energy
"I'm feeling this more deeply than you"
no one knows like no one   looks at the
                            numbers
        wanting to be smaller
take the diesel?   divorce as a function
flywheel joystick pair wrapped to go
with mustard
the last last time again

              *

      Hesitant?   Once you're in just
toss the goods down   insurance covers itself
right not to pay   don't check the second box
        final moment on the ladder

Another league to move up to
desire too strong for this old-fashioned signal
       alto-sax trills   vibraphone
contradictory version
           480 channels of noise
this week the power   next a need for sense
    "perhaps a little too much drift"
reference to the shadowy elements
an underpopulated L.A.?

     One morning you wake up a witness
transitional periods / nothing changing
        jammed into a double feature
      limited time for actual talking
looking pale under bare fluorescents
"you're from the east you might like to walk"
                      simply no more
        to say than the landscape

Sitting at home, sweating it out
a spare sort of middle-class existence
on the back end
                Restless is easy can you
do desperate?   good and goodbye   on a dime
        not the best time to fall asleep
                                total devotion to the package
crazy or greedy it's just as bad

                        *

His idea of freedom was Calvin Coolidge
draws you into the mystical undertow
or car bomb century

                        *

Who lives here anymore I
am always thinking somewhere else
not like a home don't want a home
any more than I already have
each step towards the corner
a way of stilling the consciousness fear
and that bit at a time
of passing it on
really I want
to go to parties and laugh
when a guest from Russia
throws wine on the walls
stained from last time

                        *

The quiet
precise moment keenly
portrayed
barely wants anyone in it

I get out fast
cities on my arms

*

I love the way
you call people assholes
until about time twenty-three

*

A search for god
that's what that
was about?
I could have given
you one of mine
I've got dozens left over

*

Even rich football players
get shot more when they're black

*

Or you can hand it to UPS
to go non-union around the world

*

What people don't want to feel
someone's got to write

I keep getting stuck
on what they don't say

*

Like the poet of love
I could have been

*

Oh strange new world
to have such decentered free downloads in it

*

We went to the grocery
together this afternoon
now we're having
a typical fun Friday night

*

QinHuangDao HongYue Plastic company

Address: 11#Emeishan north road,
            Qinhuangdao Economic & Technologica Development Zone,
            Qinhuangdao, Herbei, China 066004.

QinHuangDao HongYue plastic company is a complex company, which
manufacture and sell professionally plastic pipe system. The company is
specialize in producing and selling ¡°HONGYUE ¡± brand PVC-U water supply
pipes, pipe fittings; PVC-U drain pipes, pipe fittings (including solid

wall drain pipes, double layer hollow wall pipes, double layer hollow
wall inner spiral pipes, storm sewer pipes, etc); PVC-U fire
resistance cabling conduits, conduit fittings; PP-R water supply and hot-water
supply pipes and pipe fittings; PE pipes, pipes fittings, PE-Xa pipes,
PE-RT pipes; PP-R aluminum compound pipes, pipe fittings.
All productions are insured by China PING AN insurance company.

The total throughput of the company is 100,000 tons. At present, the
second period industry park of HongYue,100 mu is being constructed. The

company has many branches and offices, the sales network extends to northeast, north, south, east and northwest of China. Also exported to Russia, Korea, America, Australia and Canada.

We have strong technology strength, advanced production and strict inspection device, and the company has passed ISO9001 quality control system and ISO14001 environment management system authentication.

As part of our ongoing expansion project we are in search of competent individuals and companies, who can help us establish a medium of getting to our customers in America, Canada, Europe and Australia who buy our products, with primary duties that include receipt of funds from them.

Note that, as our agent, you will receive ten percent (10%) of whatever amount you receive for the company and the balance will be paid into an account we will avail to you. If you are interested, I would appreciate you forwarding to us the informations below;

(1)Full names:
(2)Full residential or office address:
(3)Zip/postal code:
(4)Country:
(5)Tele/cell numbers:
(6)Occupation:

You are to send these informations to us via this email address; conchen6@yahoo.com.cn

Your earliest response to this e-mail will be welcome. You will be sent an e-mail notification in less than 24 hours of your reply.

Respectfully,
Mr. Connie Chen
Chairman.

*

Introducing the Butt Buoy!
Special offer: Buy any Butt Buoy and receive a FREE Key Buoy

How the Butt Buoy came to be:

It was a hot balmy day in the Mojave Valley June 2001. My friends and I were experiencing a father's day weekend on the banks of the Colorado River. The river was unusually crowded this year. We were enjoying a cold beverage when we noticed that everyone was having a similar problem. Everyone had the same marker buoy. People were hooking up to other people's buoys!! We figured there had to be a better way to distinguish your boats marker buoy from the rest. Then out of the corner of my eye I noticed two buoys tangled together. It looked like a pair of buns bobbing on the water. I looked to my left and saw this girl in a tight bikini. I thought, what a great way to individualize your buoy, make it look like a girls bottom in a bathing suit. So instead of using plain white round markers or old gallon milk jugs, you can have a truly unique marker buoy that will stand out above the rest. On the way home I shared my idea with friends. We all shared a laugh and thought what a great way to have fun and provide a unique product to our fellow boaters. We hope you have as much fun customizing your buoy as we did designing it. Happy Boating!!!

Get your butt in the water with these playful and attention grabbing buoys!
Any style Butt Buoy for just $39.95!

*

Catatonic feedback made like a lapsed Catholic
docking points to surfers   the mail
                constant options for coupons
                                    floating up
into the sum total of vision
        racoons no
but TVs, lots   "listen mister they're our guests"
"truly impressive parasitical structure"
will you be going? Are there options
for raising it?
In case you weren't there when the news
refused to report on the issue

I've got two named fear and loathing
for sale my toad! Get my toad!
Coming to you with a service array
of methods for channeling
                          he'd never
been that irrelevant before
              and now two for the price
                          photo of a ship going down
like the whole piece these days must be performed
but legally?
                          Time to talk
about fixing the plumbing in this corroded
but somehow intact interplanet device
called "headcase" by those who won't get involved
so anyway, a plumber?   Did you call
my people in The White House Dream Room
feasibility fake-it bubble? And after all
that you want cash? Like adapting
a ticking time bomb? "We've got just the role
picked? fit? out for these poor Mexican guys
who didn't consult the fine print"
                          Want more beauty, less sociology?
        Think it's time to grade
they always want it cooked without lard
                  news, it seemed, to the subtitle industry
you're so naive about compliance
        "I've got the forms   right here I've got them"
paid through the weekend
not sure there's time to think about it
among cries for more ear candy transcendence
        your basic inquisition
        cash machines installed in each lobby

                          *

Speeds up then abruptly stops
                  time to answer a bank of questions

14

for instance, your expression resembles
a battery of received data
tilting while it throws out conclusions

      Walked the streets of the village   all five
"I do not   have a take on the statement"
people will continue to live here
     not so inspiring really
        cue the talk about overcoming
molecules in the same
      middle   same scene of usual invading
                  beasts' year end event
              usual links to starting over

     Stare at the sun treat people like a picture
        big plate of little tacos
the world's on special
profound connection to the immediate
     lessons learned: the list
will not accept splitting the difference
        Still trying to adjust to the real
the way they run it at Princeton

        *

You could try this too if you liked
          the moment, feasible
    actual customers on hidden camera
did my research
and ended up just outside Tuscaloosa
         in a rented van
      Canadians have a different way
      of shouting in the tunnel
     "It's not that you're making me mad
     it's that you think you're making me mad
     that makes me mad"–Rube Waddell
        another cut rate

end of America vision thing
haul them on down to a limiting clarity
against that rush
                        The little village
one more fringe of interlocking
ways of saying what no one believes:
here the sum total of here
                    except you failed to notice
all those people never described
        (she keeps saying,
                    "Kids eat for 99 cents")
no one finished the sentence
                distinctive sporting whoops and hollers
        they'd agree entirely elsewhere
                        entirely elsewhere
while she walks up the balcony stairs
hey there handstand yogi of love
        I toss you bits
        that make a world
        such as we have
        there is only that to offer

        and not the big scythe

                        *

Not many chances left
for unused double entendres
                        a serious man
        and his vehement protest
        that anything has another side

a ragged figure stands at the crossroads
                "Maybe not walk there"

        "Will if I want to"

                    like the traffic jam means
                    we're going freely?
To say, to choose sides
to discard a national vision
                        portend some moment soon
                            that expectation will have neglected
            "I can't see you," he said,
            looking right at them
love card home card death card
                    perfectly orchestrated crescendo
                    even during gunfire
            outside it's hard to breathe
                    and afterwards pay for delivery

                    *

learning vs. bureaucracy

                    *

thought it read "lemming"

                    *

Nothing should be
incompatible
with the life of the people

low roar freeway at night
wind passing through the barrel
            systems repair   control stop

flourishing indifference
                    as one becomes too tired becomes
                    a factor of the likeness
            recognizing the instigations
            the empty, well-kept mansion

blinds carefully closed, lawn
cut evenly to the sidewalk and watered
for the no one who sleeps there

blinking feedback causes epileptic
rotation torn from its roots

                  dialectic of the cubby
                  specialized reflection device

playing off two-way
martyr advancement prerogatives
in the asteroidal
contumely and privileged interstices
laced with "fun day" paraphernalia

        all the times
        not to be thinking like the times
        have come undone
                surprising, given the temperate winter
            hilltop land breaking
            off towards the ocean

technological, natural
last flotsam bits
floating in the comment stream
splintered the eye

            for if like one like half a dozen
            meaning no one but

        *

For instance, how TV
changes connection to the immediate
flaked-paint pickup with sign
            claiming FIREWOOD

imagining the future
information chip

powerful

sense of here as not being
real, rough balcony floor of light blue stucco

                    to be set far back
                    from the world
                    to make the world move
                    like TV
                    to make people
                    move like TV

not only does it appear to be happening

fuel that would start this engine running
pre-selection to be portrayed
this way Hollywood

                        the writer's strike: words
                        play a role in supporting the visual
                        extension into new
                        profit arenas

        hot wings without sauce
        Big Al shaking
        his booty cheering the winning
        horse who later died at the Preakness

                        absence of myself
                        standing in doors looking out

            *

Blue-lit pool
grass fades on edges of

      most days nothing
      much at stake

—the abstracted distance

              roiling

    *

"a lot less hat a lot
      more cattle"

    *

    No escape from the ideology
           is ideology
              no
              bringing back

    *

Polls are closing in the state of the mind

    *

One part insistence two
      parts removal

    *

    Distance from
    the problem is
    the problem

*

Newspapering the booster show
                         keep confusing
                         reality and real estate
         at "home" a general calm

         the price-per-unit service
         infiltrating the megashow rates
         adjustable for inflammatory
         ways to sell kit-and-kaboodle
         no rebate mercenary wars

                         fresh air, packaged
perk in the ultimate cable
option for the outskirts
         the no-city center
         strip mall side deal, rotated
                         against the girth
fertile land once sold for pennies

         conflicted biospheres among need
         in outdated poverty calculations
         (if all locales are equal in cost)

         Nobody believes
         that the actual cash-down come-on
         routine will dictate reputation
         or make sure the floor
                  is balanced

         Has anyone seen
         the new brand of inflatable
         monsters symbolizing "real human nightmares"

         in startling shapes

here in the fourth
largest suburb on the west
northwest side
of this two-bit big-beer town?

Homemade linkery directly to table
with your face
reprinted daily

       sign, then drive

   *

Looking for inner peace
economic growth
and tarantulas

   *

On emotional high alert
are those really
dogs they look like dogs, they coalesce
under the 7/11 lamplight

       some old-fashioned
       "punk rock or disco?"
       debate jamming the channels

   rising price
   of Rice Krispies and milk,

        forecloser's paradise
        among corners with tasty
        Mexican food stands
        no stories about people no
        people telling stories
        grab some eternal bliss and go

to the racetrack
doubling down on my own
new season of thrilling episodes
      "Cash Back"   "Time As Abandonment"
"The End of Efficiency"
         "Breaking the Spirit at the High School Level"
     "Flexible Mythologies"
           "Two Dollars in Quarters"
"Nothing Really Thanks"   "That Heavy Metal Ambiance"

The train blows past like this
is the last place to be

       *

Groups walk past in pairs and fours
occasional   a barefoot man
sits by the town center fountain

        in dreams the victors
        and all that follows
it's a good way to vacation
family staggers into the Honda

          really, a yellow umbrella
          and hurried walk

     the frame or the thing in the frame

     and who's writing history

make it sound
like no one's been there
I sure haven't
not in that way

the difference at the ocean

                 gather at the bicycle shop
                 it's not exactly pressure

one can only *want* so long
or so the dogs, children, and mothers

                        attest

                 didn't say you weren't the point
                 said why do you have to call it a point

                 all things not considered

September 2007 - March 2008

CPSIA information can be obtained
at www.ICGtesting.com
Printed in the USA
BVHW091218220119
538285BV00006B/189/P

9 781943 899081